"Faculty members are much more productive when they receive communications with clarity, engage in meaningful work, and have the distinct knowledge that they are cared about by their school leadership. Using the easy-to-follow steps that Teaching Excellence provides with your faculty ensures that they feel supported and encouraged in their professional growth. The book will prove to be a valuable tool in improving your school."

— *Nathan Washer, Assistant Head of School, The Pine School (FL)*

"After reading Teaching Excellence, I have a sense of renewed purpose. I want to share this book with my level team, the rest of the staff, and the administration! If we used this book to reflect on our teaching practices, and really took to heart the 13 Characteristics of Teaching Excellence as identified by ISM's research, I have no doubt that the impact on student enthusiasm, performance, and satisfaction would be significantly positive, to say the least. If we embraced using Teaching Excellence as a staff, as part of a guide to our professional development, I think it'd be impossible to not feel better about the daily work we do. Every new and veteran teacher should have a copy of the book at their fingertips. If administrators want to see great things happening in their schools, then this is a great resource to help in getting there."

— *Karen Backenstose, Teacher, The New School (PA)*

"Resulting from years of data-driven research that demonstrate how student success correlates to predictable and supportive school environments, ISM details 13 essential Teaching Characteristics. These characteristics allow teachers to assess their effectiveness as teacher leaders and hone their ability to move students to learned optimism. Practical examples of effective teaching and self-assessment tools allow teachers to reflect and grow. This workbook will prove beneficial to teachers at any stage of their teaching career, and administrators will find the Faculty Culture Profile a helpful tool to monitor their efforts in cultivating a predictable and supportive faculty culture."

— *Jason Erb, Lower School Principal/Bible Teacher, Wesleyan School (GA)*

"I became a teacher because I knew that every single child had the capability of being something wonderful, as long as there was someone who believed in them and inspired them. I became an administrator because I knew that these same students deserved to have every one of their teachers be a source of inspiration. For that to happen, great teachers need people who believe in and support them. Teaching Excellence encapsulates these feelings much more eloquently than I can, and provides clear and practical steps to help reinvigorate that original passion for teaching and create a new, meaningful pathway forward."

— *Christianna Dakin, Curriculum Director, Saltus Grammar School, Bermuda*

Teaching Excellence
A Research-Based Workbook for Teachers
Third Edition

Based on research and concepts developed by Independent School Management Consultants, past and present. Special thanks to M. Walker Buckalew, author of the original edition, and Barbara Beachley. Edited by Weldon Burge.

Disclaimer: Independent School Management, Inc., (ISM) provides management consulting and other services to private schools. ISM is not a law firm. No service or information provided by ISM in any verbal or written form (including this book) should be construed as legal advice. ISM specifically advises schools to consult with legal counsel qualified in their jurisdiction regarding all legal matters (including the hiring, rewarding, and terminating of personnel). All Web links and references in this book are correct as of the publication date, but may have become inactive or otherwise modified since that time.

Paperback ISBN-13: 978-1-883627-22-5

Contents

Overview

Independent School Management (ISM) has provided advice and counsel to private-independent schools since the mid-1970s. A data-driven organization, ISM launches research projects regularly in pursuit of various hypotheses.

This book is the result of two research projects spanning more than two decades (and more than 15 years of pertinent experience between them). One was the seminal project in its examination of factors influencing student performance, student satisfaction, and student enthusiasm. The other was a partial replication and statistical strengthening of the original project. This book treats the findings of both.

In ISM's research, a statistical correlation has been firmly established between teacher-determined classroom conditions called by ISM "predictability and supportiveness" (as perceived through the eyes of students) and student performance, student-perceived satisfaction, and student-perceived enthusiasm. These classroom conditions are not a function of pedagogical "style," teacher "personality," or age of student. These conditions can be created by the application (by teachers) of a cluster of characteristics and principles.

This volume presents these characteristics and principles in workbook form.

"Predictability and supportiveness"—the paired set of critical classroom conditions and organizational ingredients—have been found in these studies in greatest strength in school environments in which students perceive that:

- the rule and reward structure is strong, but also intelligible and fair from the student perspective;

- faculty, administration, and coaching responses are consistent, fair, and accurate from the student perspective, in regard to what is positively or negatively reinforced (academically and behaviorally); and

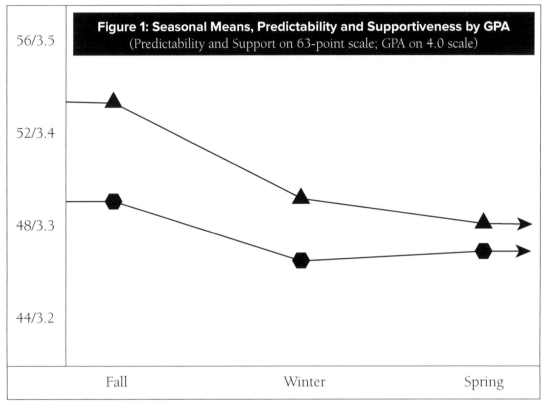

Figure 1: Seasonal Means, Predictability and Supportiveness by GPA
(Predictability and Support on 63-point scale; GPA on 4.0 scale)

56/3.5

52/3.4

48/3.3

44/3.2

Fall   Winter   Spring

Fall P&S and GPA correlation relationships significant at the .1 level
Winter/Spring P&S and GPA correlation relationships significant at the .01 level

Predictability and Support ▲   **GPA** ⬢

– the faculty, administration, and coaching staffs appear to the students to genuinely desire student success and work to elicit that success, but nonetheless provide accurate—not inflated—reinforcement (as implied by the first two items in this list).

(The measuring device for these characteristics, the Student Experience Profile, may be seen in Appendix B of this book. This instrument is designed for use by students in grades 5–12.)

A rapid-look summary of the research relationships is presented in Figures 1 and 2. In Figure 1, predictability and supportiveness levels (P&S) are shown as they were found in ISM's most recent study for fall, winter, and spring grading periods. Shown in the same figure (with a different scale along the vertical axis) are the cumulative grade-point averages (GPA) of students in the study. GPAs, as expected (based on earlier ISM findings), were highest in fall, lowest in winter, and intermediate in spring. Measures of P&S, on the other hand, were highest in fall, dropped considerably in winter, and declined further in spring.

The correlation statistic showed a significant relationship between P&S and GPA in the fall, but at the lowest traditionally acceptable level of social-science "significance" (.1). The correlation strengthened throughout the year, reaching significance levels of .01 in winter and spring. This is suggested graphically in Figure 1 by the decreasing gap between P&S measures and GPAs as the school year progresses.

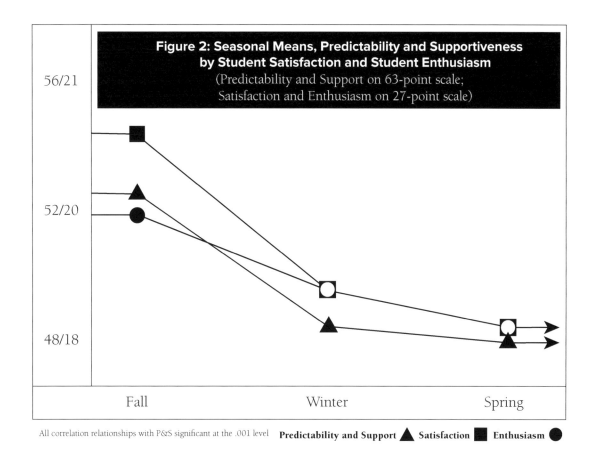

Figure 2: Seasonal Means, Predictability and Supportiveness by Student Satisfaction and Student Enthusiasm
(Predictability and Support on 63-point scale;
Satisfaction and Enthusiasm on 27-point scale)

All correlation relationships with P&S significant at the .001 level   **Predictability and Support** ▲ **Satisfaction** ■ **Enthusiasm** ●

In Figure 2, predictability and supportiveness levels (P&S) are, as in Figure 1, shown as they were found in ISM's most recent study for fall, winter, and spring grading periods. Shown in the same figure (with a different scale along the vertical axis) are student-perceived satisfaction (SAT) and student-perceived enthusiasm (ENTH) levels for each season. Measures for all of these variables declined throughout the school year.

The correlation statistic showed a highly significant relationship between P&S and SAT and between P&S and ENTH in each season of the school year. The strength of this relationship (.001), already powerful in the fall, continued to strengthen in both winter and spring grading periods. This is suggested graphically in Figure 2 by the decreasing gap between measures for P&S and SAT and between measures for P&S and ENTH as the school year progresses.

Note: Throughout this book, you will encounter the word "follower" in reference to the teacher's role relative to the leader. The use of this word is intentional to distinguish teachers as followers versus subordinates. The Analytical Center for Leadership Research and Development defines "follower as "an employee who is more of a partner than a subordinate. Follower implies the voluntary action of joining someone's agenda or goals based on shared ideals, opinions, or values. It means possessing an internal motivation to do something. In other words, voluntary followers are workers that embrace their jobs in ways that hold an intrinsic value to him or her." When a leader is not leading with predictability and support, she is more likely to have subordinates, employees who do what they are told, than to have willing followers."
(http://www.aclrd.com/subordinates-vs-followers)

Predictability and Supportiveness: The ISM Faculty Experience Matrix

A school culture strongly marked by "predictability" and "supportiveness" ("High P-High S") in the environment can be expected to display specific organizational characteristics. This can be said, as well, about the other three possible culture-pairings: high predictability and low supportiveness ("High P-Low S"); low predictability and high supportiveness ("Low P-High S"); and low predictability and low supportiveness ("Low P-Low S").

A discussion of these four quadrants and a graphic display follows.

High Predictability-High Supportiveness (High P-High S)

- Consistent and constructive faculty evaluation

- Mission-based decision-making

- Predictability and support sustained over time

- Balanced leadership (prescriptive and nonprescriptive)

- Healthy student and faculty cultures

In the "High P-High S" quadrant, each of these five items implies the other four, i.e., it is difficult to implement one of these extremely well without simultaneously doing extremely well with the others. In regard to faculty evaluation, for example, "balanced leadership" that is "both prescriptive and nonprescriptive" would often mean the administration chooses to dictate the structure, ground rules, and research base for the faculty evaluation system (thus, "prescriptive"). At the same time, the administration may choose to delegate the creation of the evaluation system's specific criteria for excellence to a faculty task unit, subject to the administration's final approval ("nonprescriptive").

Outcomes of such an approach are likely to include (a) more consistent and constructive evaluation; (b) a healthier faculty culture; and (c) a more predictable and supportive environment, as seen through the eyes of the teachers themselves. This is but one among countless possible examples of the effects of leaders' "balanced"—prescriptive and nonprescriptive—decisions on organizational process, culture, and performance.

High Predictability-Low Supportiveness (High P-Low S)

- Bureaucratic faculty evaluation

- Rules, not reasons

- Authoritarian leadership

- Culture of fear or resentment

- Conformist culture

The list above represents the (expected) major characteristics of an organization that is strong in predictability but weak in supportiveness. Such a school is weak in creating an environment in which teachers, in their relationship to administrators; and students, in their relationship to teachers, coaches, and administrators—*are confident that their leaders wish them success* (whether they are as yet successful or not). While "High P-Low S" organizations tend to develop all five of the characteristics shown above, there may be exceptions.

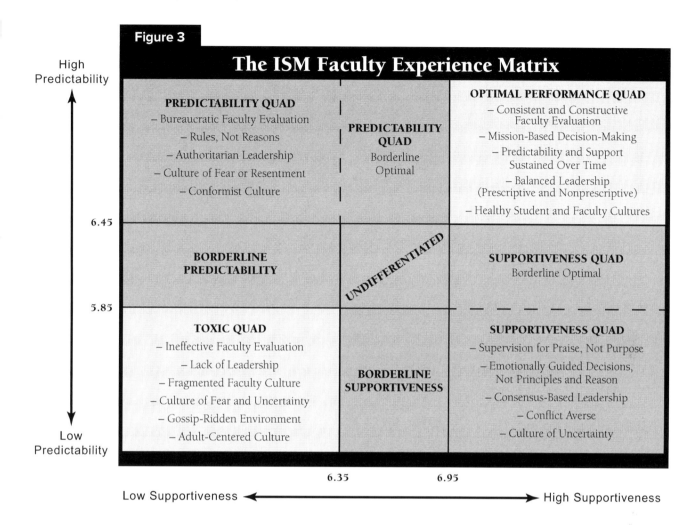

Figure 3

The ISM Faculty Experience Matrix

High Predictability

Low Predictability

PREDICTABILITY QUAD
- Bureaucratic Faculty Evaluation
- Rules, Not Reasons
- Authoritarian Leadership
- Culture of Fear or Resentment
- Conformist Culture

PREDICTABILITY QUAD
Borderline Optimal

OPTIMAL PERFORMANCE QUAD
- Consistent and Constructive Faculty Evaluation
- Mission-Based Decision-Making
- Predictability and Support Sustained Over Time
- Balanced Leadership (Prescriptive and Nonprescriptive)
- Healthy Student and Faculty Cultures

6.45

BORDERLINE PREDICTABILITY

UNDIFFERENTIATED

SUPPORTIVENESS QUAD
Borderline Optimal

5.85

TOXIC QUAD
- Ineffective Faculty Evaluation
- Lack of Leadership
- Fragmented Faculty Culture
- Culture of Fear and Uncertainty
- Gossip-Ridden Environment
- Adult-Centered Culture

BORDERLINE SUPPORTIVENESS

SUPPORTIVENESS QUAD
- Supervision for Praise, Not Purpose
- Emotionally Guided Decisions, Not Principles and Reason
- Consensus-Based Leadership
- Conflict Averse
- Culture of Uncertainty

6.35   6.95

Low Supportiveness ← → High Supportiveness

Note: The ISM Faculty Experience Matrix, Survey, Scoring Instructions, and Scoring Chart, can be found in Appendix A.

For example, an authoritarian administrator who is perceived not as "mean," but as goal-focused to the exclusion of all else, may steer clear of the worst aspects of a "culture of fear and resentment" (just as an authoritarian teacher may not consistently produce fear or resentment in students). But, without leadership attentiveness to the "supportiveness" component (producing a settled confidence on the part of the followers that the leader truly wishes their success), fear and resentment will always be a heartbeat away.

Successful military combat units are "High P-Low S" with good reason, i.e., errors can result in death to the troops themselves and, beyond that, to those whom they endeavor to protect. In contrast, in teaching and learning organizations such as schools, experimentation (such as "action research" for teachers and electronic trial-and-correction software for students) has a necessary function. It is *freedom-within-structure* that tends to foster high levels of performance, satisfaction, and enthusiasm at both the teacher and student levels. Predictability is essential, but without supportiveness, predictability is ultimately self-defeating in school contexts.

Low Predictability-High Supportiveness (Low P-High S)

- Supervision for praise, not purpose

- Emotionally guided decisions, not principles and reason

- Consensus-based leadership

- Conflict-averse

- Culture of uncertainty

This is the "natural" quadrant toward which educators—teachers and administrators—tend to gravitate. This is the case because educators are usually most comfortable in environments characterized by intellectual give-and-take within an academic society of equals. Ideas predominate and the most worthy ideas prevail.

Effective PK–12 schools for children and adolescents, however, are not graduate seminars. Schools have missions, purposes, and outcomes, coupled with paying "customers." The latter commit significant portions of their families' resources to private schools so that their children may experience those missions, purposes, and outcomes.

And this implies hierarchy. Those at or near the top of those hierarchies determine the school mission, purposes, and desired outcomes. Thus, "predictability" is established by means of organizational structures that make the mission-specific "deliverables" likely to materialize.

When this "predictability" component is given little or no meaningful attention, "supportiveness"—teachers' confidence that the administrators desire their success and students' confidence that their teachers desire their success—may reach high levels. However, without "predictability," it is likely that uncertainty and a lack of trust in the administration's leadership will eventually come to predominate among teachers. High (mission-specific) performance, high (mission-related) satisfaction, and high (mission-related) enthusiasm are the first casualties of the "Low P-High S" environment.

Low Predictability-Low Supportiveness (Low P-Low S)

- Ineffective faculty evaluation

- Lack of leadership

- Fragmented faculty culture

- Culture of fear and uncertainty

- Gossip-ridden environment

- Adult-centered culture

Where both "predictability" and "supportiveness" are in short supply, toxic environments develop, even though there may be numerous individuals who manage to avoid the toxicity. The reverse of the familiar adage, "a rising tide lifts all boats," comes inexorably into play. The prevailing "low tide" will frustrate these (often heroic) individual efforts to provide high levels of performance, satisfaction, and enthusiasm for the students.

Seldom can such toxicity be corrected without, in James Collins's memorable metaphor, "getting the wrong people off the bus and the right people on the bus and in the right seats." This does not mean that teachers should not challenge ideas or contribute their own thoughts and expertise to school discussions, which is part of a healthy school culture. It means, rather, that teachers must do this with student performance, student satisfaction, and student enthusiasm at the heart of their motivation.

Self-Directed Analysis (Part One)

There is no single "correct" way to use the material in this workbook. From this point on, the rest of this material will deal with developing the teacher-student, teacher-teacher, and teacher-administrator implications of ISM's "predictability and supportiveness" findings as they apply to your school. Here are a few of your choices.

- Work through the rest of the material as an individual. Use the workbook-like pages to score yourself, to decide about changes in your own approach that you might wish to attempt, and to set professional growth goals.

- Do the same in cooperation with one or more of your peers. Meet periodically to discuss these ideas, to initiate individual or small-group (pedagogical) trials (a form of "action research"), and to compare notes week-by-week and month-by-month.

- Involve your administrator(s) to:

   (a) perform a whole-faculty self-scoring on the ISM Faculty Experience Survey Instrument and Scoring Chart (Appendix A);

   (b) discuss the outcomes vis-à-vis the ISM Faculty Experience Matrix (shown in the previous chapter);

   (c) administer the Student Experience Profile (Appendix B);

   (d) administer the Faculty Culture Profile (Appendix C);

(e) incorporate some element of the Characteristics of Teaching Excellence into your growth and renewal plan; and

(f) in other creative ways, integrate your own work in this book with the in-parallel work of your colleagues. Do this with the long-term goal of establishing and maintaining your faculty culture's position in the upper-right quadrant of the ISM Faculty Experience Matrix.

The material following in this chapter is designed to address the question of how your current approach to teaching "plays" in the context of ISM's findings on the student experience. The 13 "Characteristics of Teaching Excellence" presented in this chapter were found in ISM's Student Experience Study to have a statistical relationship to student performance, student satisfaction, and student enthusiasm. (Chapter Three will present a second tier of 22 related characteristics.)

Use these pages as your workbook. Respond to the rating scales that are provided, make notes in the margins, converse about the items with your peers.

Four rating scales are provided for each of the 13 characteristics. You may choose to respond only to the first scale in each case (the one referring to your current approach). The other scales will allow you to record your aspirations, your entire faculty's "averaged" ratings (in your own estimation), and your entire faculty's *range* of approaches (again, of course, in your own estimation).

The scale is one through nine, nine being "high" on each item.

Teaching Characteristic One

*I find ways to make it obvious to all students that
I wish them success every day, in and outside school.*

My Current Level

1	2	3	4	5	6	7	8	9
(Not at all)								*(At highest levels)*

My Three-Year Goal

1	2	3	4	5	6	7	8	9
(Not at all)								*(At highest levels)*

My Estimate of Our Faculty Average

1	2	3	4	5	6	7	8	9
(Not at all)								*(At highest levels)*

My Estimate of Our Faculty Range (use brackets)

1	2	3	4	5	6	7	8	9
(Not at all)								*(At highest levels)*

Comment: This is a statement *not* about your personal and professional demeanor, e.g., warm, welcoming, upbeat, or cold, standoffish, downbeat. It is a statement about your pedagogical technique—i.e., about the act of setting high expectations and making them clear (see Characteristics No. 3 and 4, following) *and* of communicating by words and actions your determination to assist the students in reaching those expectations.

Teaching Characteristic Two

I find ways to make it obvious to all students that I want them to become better, more ethical people (in ways consistent with our school's stated purposes and projected outcomes for our graduates).

My Current Level

1	2	3	4	5	6	7	8	9
(Not at all)								*(At highest levels)*

My Three-Year Goal

1	2	3	4	5	6	7	8	9
(Not at all)								*(At highest levels)*

My Estimate of Our Faculty Average

1	2	3	4	5	6	7	8	9
(Not at all)								*(At highest levels)*

My Estimate of Our Faculty Range (use brackets)

1	2	3	4	5	6	7	8	9
(Not at all)								*(At highest levels)*

Comment: This is a statement *not* about your commitment to the school mission—which is assumed—but about your willingness and ability to make this commitment overt. Since mission statements implicitly or explicitly assert the school's intention to develop good people and good citizens, your "public" references to, and insistence upon, ethical conduct (e.g., conduct that exemplifies truth, honesty, integrity, and fair play) comprise core characteristics of teaching excellence.

Teaching Characteristic Three

I set clearly articulated standards for student academic performance.

My Current Level

1	2	3	4	5	6	7	8	9
(Not at all)								*(At highest levels)*

My Three-Year Goal

1	2	3	4	5	6	7	8	9
(Not at all)								*(At highest levels)*

My Estimate of Our Faculty Average

1	2	3	4	5	6	7	8	9
(Not at all)								*(At highest levels)*

My Estimate of Our Faculty Range (use brackets)

1	2	3	4	5	6	7	8	9
(Not at all)								*(At highest levels)*

Comment: This is a statement *not* about your own scoring and grading system itself, but about your ability and willingness to illuminate the nature of your academic expectations, i.e., *not* about explaining that 90–93 = A- and 94–97 = A and 98–100 = A+, but delineating (in age-appropriate fashion, of course) the subject-specific levels of mastery that you expect from your students. An illustration of this might entail providing students with examples (in advance of an assignment) of submissions that you would grade as A, B, C, and so on, or involving your students in the development of the rubric.

Teaching Characteristic Four

I set reasonable, defensible standards for student behavior.

My Current Level

| 1 | 2 | 3 | 4 | 5 | 6 | 7 | 8 | 9 |

(Not at all)   *(At highest levels)*

My Three-Year Goal

| 1 | 2 | 3 | 4 | 5 | 6 | 7 | 8 | 9 |

(Not at all)   *(At highest levels)*

My Estimate of Our Faculty Average

| 1 | 2 | 3 | 4 | 5 | 6 | 7 | 8 | 9 |

(Not at all)   *(At highest levels)*

My Estimate of Our Faculty Range (use brackets)

| 1 | 2 | 3 | 4 | 5 | 6 | 7 | 8 | 9 |

(Not at all)   *(At highest levels)*

Comment: This is a statement *not* about schoolwide rules and regulations, but about the behavioral expectations you develop for students in your own classroom. The statement implies that your behavioral expectations should be spelled out—possibly in writing and posted in your classroom—and, beyond that, should be explained in ways that are intelligible to your students. (It is worth remembering that "bad laws make hard cases." Your standards for student behavior in your classroom should relate to the school mission and should be viewed by students as *reasonable* applications of that mission.) As a community-building opportunity at the beginning of the year, consider involving your students in the development of classroom rules, etiquette, and expectations.

Teaching Characteristic Five

I am continually alert to displays of unkindness among students.

My Current Level

1	2	3	4	5	6	7	8	9
(Near zero)								*(At highest levels)*

My Three-Year Goal

1	2	3	4	5	6	7	8	9
(Near zero)								*(At highest levels)*

My Estimate of Our Faculty Average

1	2	3	4	5	6	7	8	9
(Near zero)								*(At highest levels)*

My Estimate of Our Faculty Range (use brackets)

1	2	3	4	5	6	7	8	9
(Near zero)								*(At highest levels)*

Comment: This statement references your alertness to a widespread and pervasive threat to the fabric of any healthy student culture. "Mean" students—who may, in fact, be "mean" in no other ways—may tend to "pick on" other students in subtle ways, even *during* teacher-centered class sessions, and in not-so-subtle ways during small-group work, in hallways, in bathrooms, before or after school, or at other times when the focus of your attention is not specifically on all unkind acts. You can heighten your sensitivity to this culture-destroying phenomenon and, working with your colleagues, develop more effective methods—both classroom-specific and schoolwide—of combating it with social-emtional learning and inclusion programs.

Teaching Characteristic Six

In confrontations with students, I conduct myself in ways that leave students' dignity intact regardless of the nature of the issue or infraction.

My Current Level

1	2	3	4	5	6	7	8	9
(Never)								(Always)

My Three-Year Goal

1	2	3	4	5	6	7	8	9
(Never)								(Always)

My Estimate of Our Faculty Average

1	2	3	4	5	6	7	8	9
(Never)								(Always)

My Estimate of Our Faculty Range (use brackets)

1	2	3	4	5	6	7	8	9
(Never)								(Always)

Comment: Confrontations with certain students may be inevitable. This statement underscores the importance of developing the skill-set to conduct a confrontation without in any way demeaning the student(s) being confronted. For most teachers, implementing this Teaching Characteristic successfully implies (a) a steady focus during the confrontation on the unacceptable *actions* of the student, rather than on the student's personality or character; and (b) learning to create opportunities for inclusion that can be delivered as soon after the confrontation as realistically possible, e.g., "Is that absolutely clear, then? Yes? Good … now, will you help Elise and Jason get these papers ready for distribution? Thank you."

Teaching Characteristic Seven

I demonstrate believably high levels of enthusiasm for teaching and learning and for the content of my studies.

My Current Level

1	2	3	4	5	6	7	8	9
(Not at all)								*(At highest levels)*

My Three-Year Goal

1	2	3	4	5	6	7	8	9
(Not at all)								*(At highest levels)*

My Estimate of Our Faculty Average

1	2	3	4	5	6	7	8	9
(Not at all)								*(At highest levels)*

My Estimate of Our Faculty Range (use brackets)

1	2	3	4	5	6	7	8	9
(Not at all)								*(At highest levels)*

Comment: This statement is *not* one that is made in reference to your "personality" (an elusive concept in any case). The statement deals, rather, with the extent to which you are able to give evidence—by your words and actions—to your students that (a) you are eager for them to learn the material, (b) you are gratified when they do, and (c) you find the content of your academic material of real (potential) significance to them. (Note: If your "current level"—as reflected in the self-rating above—is quite low, this should serve as a warning signal to you that, barring a meaningful experience of professional renewal, the time may have come for you to retire or to move to another career.)

Teaching Characteristic Eight

*I demonstrate through words and actions a genuine, believable commitment
to the school, its purposes, its leadership, and my peers.*

My Current Level

1	2	3	4	5	6	7	8	9
(Not at all)								(At highest levels)

My Three-Year Goal

1	2	3	4	5	6	7	8	9
(Not at all)								(At highest levels)

My Estimate of Our Faculty Average

1	2	3	4	5	6	7	8	9
(Not at all)								(At highest levels)

My Estimate of Our Faculty Range (use brackets)

1	2	3	4	5	6	7	8	9
(Not at all)								(At highest levels)

Comment: Your students' individual and collective commitments, or lack thereof, to your school, its purposes, and its personnel can be expected, in part, to reflect your own. Slighting verbal or nonverbal references on your part—in front of students—to the institution, its mission, or its people *will* influence students' attitudes and behaviors (and thus, their performance, satisfaction, and enthusiasm). This item is a "pure" teaching characteristic. To fail here is not merely to fall short in areas of recommended instructional approaches, but to behave in ways that are actually unprofessional. There are consequences for the *students*.

Teaching Characteristic Nine

I am glad to arrive at school and to see my students each day.

My Current Level

1	2	3	4	5	6	7	8	9

(Not at all)   (At highest levels)

My Three-Year Goal

1	2	3	4	5	6	7	8	9

(Not at all)   (At highest levels)

My Estimate of Our Faculty Average

1	2	3	4	5	6	7	8	9

(Not at all)   (At highest levels)

My Estimate of Our Faculty Range (use brackets)

1	2	3	4	5	6	7	8	9

(Not at all)   (At highest levels)

Comment: A teacher displaying the opposite of this characteristic will not *necessarily* appear angry, surly, or sullen upon her or his daily arrival at school. (No school employee consistently displaying those qualities will be long employed.) The "real-life" opposite of this characteristic describes a teacher who arrives at school appearing consistently unmotivated, morose, or distracted. These qualities are translated by students—often correctly—as suggesting the teacher's lack of enthusiasm not merely for teaching as a meaningful activity, but that teacher's lack of enthusiasm for the students themselves. As with the previous item, your conduct and your demeanor have consequences for *student* performance, satisfaction, and enthusiasm.

Teaching Characteristic Ten

I create predictable assessments (not to be confused either with "simple" or "easy" assessments). My students can rely on the preparation that I offer them.

My Current Level

1	2	3	4	5	6	7	8	9
(Not at all)								*(At highest levels)*

My Three-Year Goal

1	2	3	4	5	6	7	8	9
(Not at all)								*(At highest levels)*

My Estimate of Our Faculty Average

1	2	3	4	5	6	7	8	9
(Not at all)								*(At highest levels)*

My Estimate of Our Faculty Range (use brackets)

1	2	3	4	5	6	7	8	9
(Not at all)								*(At highest levels)*

Comment: This statement emphasizes the principle that assessments of any sort should reveal each student's grasp of facts, concepts, and their applications in problem-solving contexts, *not* their abilities either to guess what the teacher means, to deal with unexpected testing formats, or to retrieve material that was not cited in assignments or in the review process. One of the surest ways to reduce levels of student performance, satisfaction, and enthusiasm is to assess students in ways that leave them consistently feeling "tricked." Students should feel, receiving their grade, that they had been told what format to expect, what material would be included, and the teacher's expectations (see Teaching Characteristic No. 3, "Comment"). While authentic assessments that require students to demonstrate learned skills in new contexts are excellent learning tools, students should know ahead of time that they will be asked to do this (if the context itself is not known), and they should have had plenty of low-stakes practice applying skills to new contexts prior to the graded assessment.

Teaching Characteristic Eleven

I provide fair, reliable, understandable grade and reward structures for my students. My students are led to understand why they receive the grades they receive—high or low—and thereby to see how improvement, if they will seek it, might be possible.

My Current Level

1	2	3	4	5	6	7	8	9
(Not at all)								(At highest levels)

My Three-Year Goal

1	2	3	4	5	6	7	8	9
(Not at all)								(At highest levels)

My Estimate of Our Faculty Average

1	2	3	4	5	6	7	8	9
(Not at all)								(At highest levels)

My Estimate of Our Faculty Range (use brackets)

1	2	3	4	5	6	7	8	9
(Not at all)								(At highest levels)

Comment: While the words "fair," "reliable," and "understandable" connote this Teaching Characteristic's transparent relationship to "predictability," its relationship to "supportiveness" is even more critical. The simplest way to say this is that your feedback to your students on anything that is graded should leave them feeling *hopeful* that improvement might be possible. Your explicit comments—written or oral—on the steps needed to improve are considerably more important than the grade itself in this process. While the "improvement ball" always remains in your students' court, so to speak, the teacher's role must always include further instructions on the grip, the swing, the tactics, and the strategy. The least *and* the most academically successful of your students must feel an unquestioning confidence that you expect them to get better, from the first day of school to the last.

Teaching Characteristic Twelve

I enforce the school's rules justly, fairly, and consistently.

My Current Level

1	2	3	4	5	6	7	8	9
(Not at all)								*(At highest levels)*

My Three-Year Goal

1	2	3	4	5	6	7	8	9
(Not at all)								*(At highest levels)*

My Estimate of Our Faculty Average

1	2	3	4	5	6	7	8	9
(Not at all)								*(At highest levels)*

My Estimate of Our Faculty Range (use brackets)

1	2	3	4	5	6	7	8	9
(Not at all)								*(At highest levels)*

Comment: You may wish to review the "Comment" under Teaching Characteristic No. 4. That characteristic dealt with setting specific behavioral expectations and standards for your own students in your own classroom, i.e., expectations and standards that promote your particular approach to the teaching and learning equation. Teaching Characteristic No. 12, on the other hand, deals with schoolwide rules for behavior and appearance. You must be as "predictable" vis-à-vis these rules as with your own teaching and learning-specific ones. As noted in No. 4's "Comment," it is a fact that "bad laws make hard cases." When you are saddled with "bad laws" (i.e., schoolwide rules that strike you and your students as arbitrary or unnecessary), you cannot pretend they do not exist, nor can you attend to them selectively. Beyond individual consistency, it is important that *all* teachers apply the same rules in the same way. If one teacher negatively reinforces a behavior that another overlooks, a culture perceived as "unfair" by both students and teachers can develop.

Teaching Characteristic Thirteen

I am able to present myself each day in ways that will be seen by my students as consistent and reliable (i.e., unaffected by outside-of-school problems).

My Current Level

1	2	3	4	5	6	7	8	9

(Not at all)   *(At highest levels)*

My Three-Year Goal

1	2	3	4	5	6	7	8	9

(Not at all)   *(At highest levels)*

My Estimate of Our Faculty Average

1	2	3	4	5	6	7	8	9

(Not at all)   *(At highest levels)*

My Estimate of Our Faculty Range (use brackets)

1	2	3	4	5	6	7	8	9

(Not at all)   *(At highest levels)*

Comment: There are times when this characteristic will pose significant challenges. There are two guidelines to observe: (1) if the issues are so weighty that you cannot rise above them while with your students, stay home; and (2) do **not** attempt to gain sympathy from students by sharing your issues with them in detail. You may find—or have already found—that going through your regular school day thoroughly focused on your students and on the teaching and learning process is, in itself, an effective method of coping with outside-of-school issues. But however you may choose to approach this situation, your job is to be "the same" person—in terms of your demeanor, your concentration, your enthusiasm, your dedication—each day, regardless of events in your personal life. Students must be able to count on the emotional and behavioral steadiness of their instructors. Their own lives are filled with uncertainties. You must not become an additional one.

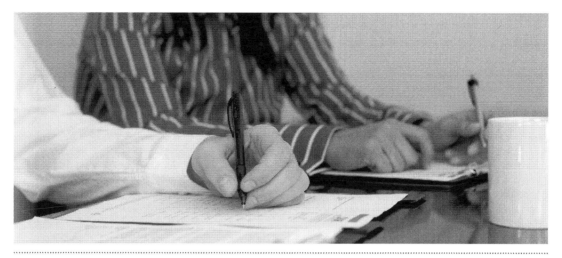

Self-Directed Analysis (Part Two)

As you did with the items in Chapter Two, you should use the pages following as a workbook. Respond to the rating scales that are provided, make notes in the margins, converse about the items with your peers. Four rating scales are provided for each of the 22 characteristics. You may choose to respond only to the first scale in each case (the one referring to your current approach). The other scales will allow you to record your aspirations, your entire faculty's "averaged" ratings (in your own estimation), and your entire faculty's *range* of approaches (again, of course, in your own estimation).

The scale is one through nine, nine being "high" on each item.

Teaching Characteristic Fourteen

I pursue career-long professional development as a foremost priority.

My Current Level

1	2	3	4	5	6	7	8	9

(Not at all)   (At highest levels)

My Three-Year Goal

1	2	3	4	5	6	7	8	9

(Not at all)   (At highest levels)

My Estimate of Our Faculty Average

1	2	3	4	5	6	7	8	9

(Not at all)   (At highest levels)

My Estimate of Our Faculty Range (use brackets)

1	2	3	4	5	6	7	8	9

(Not at all)   (At highest levels)

Teaching Characteristic Fifteen

I am current and knowledgeable about pedagogical science and my content area.

My Current Level

1	2	3	4	5	6	7	8	9
(Not at all)								(At highest levels)

My Three-Year Goal

1	2	3	4	5	6	7	8	9
(Not at all)								(At highest levels)

My Estimate of Our Faculty Average

1	2	3	4	5	6	7	8	9
(Not at all)								(At highest levels)

My Estimate of Our Faculty Range (use brackets)

1	2	3	4	5	6	7	8	9
(Not at all)								(At highest levels)

Teaching Characteristic Sixteen

I have mastered at least one pedagogical approach that is supported by reliable, contemporary research outcomes.

My Current Level

1	2	3	4	5	6	7	8	9
(Not at all)								*(At highest levels)*

My Three-Year Goal

1	2	3	4	5	6	7	8	9
(Not at all)								*(At highest levels)*

My Estimate of Our Faculty Average

1	2	3	4	5	6	7	8	9
(Not at all)								*(At highest levels)*

My Estimate of Our Faculty Range (use brackets)

1	2	3	4	5	6	7	8	9
(Not at all)								*(At highest levels)*

Teaching Characteristic Seventeen

I am effective in establishing meaningful emotional and psychological engagement with all my students.

My Current Level

1	2	3	4	5	6	7	8	9

(Not at all)   (At highest levels)

My Three-Year Goal

1	2	3	4	5	6	7	8	9

(Not at all)   (At highest levels)

My Estimate of Our Faculty Average

1	2	3	4	5	6	7	8	9

(Not at all)   (At highest levels)

My Estimate of Our Faculty Range (use brackets)

1	2	3	4	5	6	7	8	9

(Not at all)   (At highest levels)

Teaching Characteristic Eighteen

I am effective in finding creative and appropriate ways
to be involved with my students outside the classroom.

My Current Level

1	2	3	4	5	6	7	8	9
(Not at all)								(At highest levels)

My Three-Year Goal

1	2	3	4	5	6	7	8	9
(Not at all)								(At highest levels)

My Estimate of Our Faculty Average

1	2	3	4	5	6	7	8	9
(Not at all)								(At highest levels)

My Estimate of Our Faculty Range (use brackets)

1	2	3	4	5	6	7	8	9
(Not at all)								(At highest levels)

Teaching Characteristic Nineteen

I am effective in displaying an overt, conspicuous interest in students' outside-the-classroom lives—apart from the previous item—without crossing privacy boundaries.

My Current Level

1	2	3	4	5	6	7	8	9
(Not at all)								(At highest levels)

My Three-Year Goal

1	2	3	4	5	6	7	8	9
(Not at all)								(At highest levels)

My Estimate of Our Faculty Average

1	2	3	4	5	6	7	8	9
(Not at all)								(At highest levels)

My Estimate of Our Faculty Range (use brackets)

1	2	3	4	5	6	7	8	9
(Not at all)								(At highest levels)

Teaching Characteristic Twenty

I am effective in applying any subject matter to real-life conditions beyond the classroom, including applications that may be global or universal in their potential.

My Current Level

1	2	3	4	5	6	7	8	9
(Not at all)								(At highest levels)

My Three-Year Goal

1	2	3	4	5	6	7	8	9
(Not at all)								(At highest levels)

My Estimate of Our Faculty Average

1	2	3	4	5	6	7	8	9
(Not at all)								(At highest levels)

My Estimate of Our Faculty Range (use brackets)

1	2	3	4	5	6	7	8	9
(Not at all)								(At highest levels)

Teaching Characteristic Twenty-One

*I am effective in providing private and public positive
reinforcement for individual or group (student) successes.*

My Current Level

1	2	3	4	5	6	7	8	9
(Not at all)								*(At highest levels)*

My Three-Year Goal

1	2	3	4	5	6	7	8	9
(Not at all)								*(At highest levels)*

My Estimate of Our Faculty Average

1	2	3	4	5	6	7	8	9
(Not at all)								*(At highest levels)*

My Estimate of Our Faculty Range (use brackets)

1	2	3	4	5	6	7	8	9
(Not at all)								*(At highest levels)*

Teaching Characteristic Twenty-Two

I am effective in giving active support for, and establishing active engagement with, my colleagues.

My Current Level

1	2	3	4	5	6	7	8	9
(Not at all)								*(At highest levels)*

My Three-Year Goal

1	2	3	4	5	6	7	8	9
(Not at all)								*(At highest levels)*

My Estimate of Our Faculty Average

1	2	3	4	5	6	7	8	9
(Not at all)								*(At highest levels)*

My Estimate of Our Faculty Range (use brackets)

1	2	3	4	5	6	7	8	9
(Not at all)								*(At highest levels)*

Teaching Characteristic Twenty-Three

I am effective in making positive contributions to a professional, mission-focused sense of community with all constituent groups.

My Current Level

1	2	3	4	5	6	7	8	9
(Not at all)								*(At highest levels)*

My Three-Year Goal

1	2	3	4	5	6	7	8	9
(Not at all)								*(At highest levels)*

My Estimate of Our Faculty Average

1	2	3	4	5	6	7	8	9
(Not at all)								*(At highest levels)*

My Estimate of Our Faculty Range (use brackets)

1	2	3	4	5	6	7	8	9
(Not at all)								*(At highest levels)*

Teaching Characteristic Twenty-Four

I am effective in establishing proactive communication with, and service to, each student's parents.

My Current Level

	2	3	4	5	6	7	8	9
(Not at all)								(At highest levels)

My Three-Year Goal

	2	3	4	5	6	7	8	9
(Not at all)								(At highest levels)

My Estimate of Our Faculty Average

	2	3	4	5	6	7	8	9
(Not at all)								(At highest levels)

My Estimate of Our Faculty Range (use brackets)

	2	3	4	5	6	7	8	9
(Not at all)								(At highest levels)

Teaching Characteristic Twenty-Five

I am effective in making an overt commitment to the personal and professional well-being of my colleagues, administrators, and (other) nonteaching staff.

My Current Level

1	2	3	4	5	6	7	8	9
(Not at all)								*(At highest levels)*

My Three-Year Goal

1	2	3	4	5	6	7	8	9
(Not at all)								*(At highest levels)*

My Estimate of Our Faculty Average

1	2	3	4	5	6	7	8	9
(Not at all)								*(At highest levels)*

My Estimate of Our Faculty Range (use brackets)

1	2	3	4	5	6	7	8	9
(Not at all)								*(At highest levels)*

Teaching Characteristic Twenty-Six

I am effective in giving public support for my students,
my colleagues, and my employers (administration and Board).

My Current Level

1	2	3	4	5	6	7	8	9
(Not at all)								(At highest levels)

My Three-Year Goal

1	2	3	4	5	6	7	8	9
(Not at all)								(At highest levels)

My Estimate of Our Faculty Average

1	2	3	4	5	6	7	8	9
(Not at all)								(At highest levels)

My Estimate of Our Faculty Range (use brackets)

1	2	3	4	5	6	7	8	9
(Not at all)								(At highest levels)

Teaching Characteristic Twenty-Seven

*I am effective in communicating in-class experimentation-and-assessment
outcomes and findings to colleagues within and beyond the school.*

My Current Level

1	2	3	4	5	6	7	8	9
(Not at all)								*(At highest levels)*

My Three-Year Goal

1	2	3	4	5	6	7	8	9
(Not at all)								*(At highest levels)*

My Estimate of Our Faculty Average

1	2	3	4	5	6	7	8	9
(Not at all)								*(At highest levels)*

My Estimate of Our Faculty Range (use brackets)

1	2	3	4	5	6	7	8	9
(Not at all)								*(At highest levels)*

Teaching Characteristic Twenty-Eight

*I participate regularly in outside-the-school academic organizations
whose work is supportive of, and pertinent to, my field(s).*

My Current Level

1	2	3	4	5	6	7	8	9
(Not at all)								(At highest levels)

My Three-Year Goal

1	2	3	4	5	6	7	8	9
(Not at all)								(At highest levels)

My Estimate of Our Faculty Average

1	2	3	4	5	6	7	8	9
(Not at all)								(At highest levels)

My Estimate of Our Faculty Range (use brackets)

1	2	3	4	5	6	7	8	9
(Not at all)								(At highest levels)

(Items 29–35 pertain to schools with religious missions)

Teaching Characteristic Twenty-Nine

I am effective in making an overt commitment to the life of my own congregation (church, synagogue, etc.) and its core traditions.

My Current Level

1	2	3	4	5	6	7	8	9
(Not at all)								*(At highest levels)*

My Three-Year Goal

1	2	3	4	5	6	7	8	9
(Not at all)								*(At highest levels)*

My Estimate of Our Faculty Average

1	2	3	4	5	6	7	8	9
(Not at all)								*(At highest levels)*

My Estimate of Our Faculty Range (use brackets)

1	2	3	4	5	6	7	8	9
(Not at all)								*(At highest levels)*

Teaching Characteristic Thirty

I am effective in serving as a mature role model for a spiritually observant lifestyle.

My Current Level

1	2	3	4	5	6	7	8	9
(Not at all)								*(At highest levels)*

My Three-Year Goal

1	2	3	4	5	6	7	8	9
(Not at all)								*(At highest levels)*

My Estimate of Our Faculty Average

1	2	3	4	5	6	7	8	9
(Not at all)								*(At highest levels)*

My Estimate of Our Faculty Range (use brackets)

1	2	3	4	5	6	7	8	9
(Not at all)								*(At highest levels)*

Teaching Characteristic Thirty-One

I am effective in articulating the personal and ethical implications of a lifelong faith commitment.

My Current Level

1	2	3	4	5	6	7	8	9
(Not at all)								(At highest levels)

My Three-Year Goal

1	2	3	4	5	6	7	8	9
(Not at all)								(At highest levels)

My Estimate of Our Faculty Average

1	2	3	4	5	6	7	8	9
(Not at all)								(At highest levels)

My Estimate of Our Faculty Range (use brackets)

1	2	3	4	5	6	7	8	9
(Not at all)								(At highest levels)

Teaching Characteristic Thirty-Two

*I am effective in displaying appropriate levels of public
tolerance of, and respect for, other religious points of view.*

My Current Level

1	2	3	4	5	6	7	8	9
(Not at all)								(At highest levels)

My Three-Year Goal

1	2	3	4	5	6	7	8	9
(Not at all)								(At highest levels)

My Estimate of Our Faculty Average

1	2	3	4	5	6	7	8	9
(Not at all)								(At highest levels)

My Estimate of Our Faculty Range (use brackets)

1	2	3	4	5	6	7	8	9
(Not at all)								(At highest levels)

Teaching Characteristic Thirty-Three

I am knowledgeable about the developmental history of my school's religious heritage.

My Current Level

1	2	3	4	5	6	7	8	9
(Not at all)								*(At highest levels)*

My Three-Year Goal

1	2	3	4	5	6	7	8	9
(Not at all)								*(At highest levels)*

My Estimate of Our Faculty Average

1	2	3	4	5	6	7	8	9
(Not at all)								*(At highest levels)*

My Estimate of Our Faculty Range (use brackets)

1	2	3	4	5	6	7	8	9
(Not at all)								*(At highest levels)*

Teaching Characteristic Thirty-Four

*I am effective in participating in (and when appropriate, leading) the
explicitly religious components of the school's student and community programs.*

My Current Level

1	2	3	4	5	6	7	8	9
(Not at all)								(At highest levels)

My Three-Year Goal

1	2	3	4	5	6	7	8	9
(Not at all)								(At highest levels)

My Estimate of Our Faculty Average

1	2	3	4	5	6	7	8	9
(Not at all)								(At highest levels)

My Estimate of Our Faculty Range (use brackets)

1	2	3	4	5	6	7	8	9
(Not at all)								(At highest levels)

Teaching Characteristic Thirty-Five

I am committed to growing professionally and personally
within the framework of my religious traditions.

My Current Level

1	2	3	4	5	6	7	8	9
(Not at all)								*(At highest levels)*

My Three-Year Goal

1	2	3	4	5	6	7	8	9
(Not at all)								*(At highest levels)*

My Estimate of Our Faculty Average

1	2	3	4	5	6	7	8	9
(Not at all)								*(At highest levels)*

My Estimate of Our Faculty Range (use brackets)

1	2	3	4	5	6	7	8	9
(Not at all)								*(At highest levels)*

Teachers as Leaders

Many of the most high-impact characteristics of teachers (those whose approaches are associated with high levels of student performance, satisfaction, and enthusiasm) are also characteristics found in common with contemporary views of good leadership.

What are some of those characteristics? They may include:

- knowledge and expertise, which are readily perceived (*by followers*);
- a drive to stay "current" in relevant fields;
- repeatedly articulated (*to followers*) standards for performance and conduct;
- a "results" orientation;
- a "vision" of the process and the end product (and the ability and willingness to describe that vision *to followers*, often and well);
- a facility for infusing routine activities with meaning;
- a passion for preparation;
- flexibility, especially in design and evaluation;
- humility and compassion (as perceived *by followers*);
- a knack for confronting without being demeaning;
- the ability to teach (not merely assign) "responsibility"; and
- constant attention to reinforcement principles (feedback).

These ideas are not different from many of the ones expressed by a number of the Characteristics of Teaching Excellence as listed in the "Self-Directed Analysis" Chapters Two and Three. Many of these leadership characteristics represent sets of ideas identical to those in the aforementioned chapters, but usually couched in terms reserved for books and articles on leadership.

Are good leadership and good teaching "the same thing"? Not exactly. *But in those schools in which student performance, satisfaction, and enthusiasm levels are strong, teaching approaches in general are strikingly consistent with recognized "good leadership" characteristics.*

The late John W. Gardner, preeminent author and role model in the field, wrote that those in leadership too often think that their positions on the organizational chart gives them a body of "followers" (in this case, of "students") in more than name only. In fact, Gardner noted, leaders' organizational positions only give them "subordinates." These subordinates may or may not become followers, depending on whether their leaders become leaders. (Most of these thoughts closely parallel discussions he contributed to *Leadership: An Overview,* one of a series of papers prepared for the Leadership Studies Program sponsored by Independent Sector.)

Leadership, Gardner noted, is not the same as status, power, or authority. It is a process of organizing, persuading, and exemplifying that ultimately results in creation or modification of followers' knowledge, behaviors, attitudes, and habits. Leaders bestow psychological rewards—positive and negative reinforcement—*in such a way as to increase followers' sense of hope, confidence, and belief in the efficacy of their own efforts*. Above all, leaders set conditions within their own organizations that foster a sense of continuous renewal.

Reflect on your current teaching situation. To what extent are your in-class imperfections and difficulties a result of your assuming that your status as a teacher gives you "followers"? Several examples of *not* holding that assumption—examples of "good teacher and leader behavior"— follow. You will find an example from each of three levels—lower, middle, and upper school.

1. **Lower-school teacher Jones** understands that eliciting the highest (realistically attainable) performance from her students will necessitate "converting" not only her students but her students' parents, as well, to the school's views on third-graders' goals, standards, and expectations. To accomplish that, she must be convincing in front of the children and, beyond that, actually demonstrate—in person, by phone, or in emails—to their parents that she is:

   – broadly knowledgeable, astute, and academically current, ideally via actual face-to-face meetings with the children's parents;

   – articulate regarding a set of clear and exciting (to students and parents) expectations for these children's progress during this school year;

   – articulate regarding a set of clear and realistic expectations of the students' parents' roles in assisting their children in meeting the expectations for each child in her class, a set of expectations that will include written guidelines, procedures, and objectives for the parents;

   – *personally excited by, visibly passionate about, and unswervingly committed to* helping these children experience a daily sense of accomplishment that is grounded in *real progress* (as distinct from the students' being led to "feel good about themselves"—an emotional status independent of such real progress); and

   – kind, compassionate, and supportive both of children and parents, a leader who can and who obviously does empathize with her two sets of followers.

2. **Middle-school teacher Escobar** understands that eliciting the highest (realistically attainable) performance from each of his students will require him to achieve a finely adjusted balance between these young people's overwhelming need to be treated "like adults" and their bouncing-off-the-walls volatility. To find and maintain that balance, he will need to:

    – master the art of confronting-without-demeaning, and *expect to practice that art daily*;

    – demonstrate his presumably considerable subject-area(s) mastery in ways that simultaneously impress the young people and honor their (self-described) adult-like mental capacities;

    – pour huge amounts of time into preparation *to achieve flexibility* (rather than rigidity) in his daily instructional designs, thereby maintaining the ability to *lead* in a well-planned way in any of several directions, even during a single class period;

    – integrate into that preparation time effective ways of "making the routine meaningful" to pubescent human beings, partly by articulating and embodying the honest excitement he has for his field and partly by using choice-within-structure classroom techniques; and

    – attend with special care to his "results orientation" with regular, carefully articulated statements and written reminders of the expectations he has formulated for each student by year-end.

3. **Upper-school teacher Kandahar** understands that inspiring the highest (realistically attainable) performance from her students will require focused attention to content and theory in her academic field(s), coupled with a strong dose in equal measure of these psychologically difficult-to-combine conditions: high standards and difficult-to-reach goals for the students, on the one hand, and powerful instructional and personal support for the students as they work toward those goals, on the other. In working to establish these conditions, she will need to:

    – demonstrate the currency of her expertise and knowledge, citing this year's groundbreaking development in her field, this month's published report, yesterday's news release;

    – expect that with content being ubiquitous and easy for students to access, they may often know something she does not. She must use the opportunities to demonstrate humility and life-long learning;

    – couple that demonstrating-of-expertise with an oft-stated "leaderly vision" of the future, both for developments in her field, and for her students (as those developments hold potential for their futures)—for example, envisioning for and with her students the implications of current technology for language-learning, for written communication, for mathematical computation and application, for physics and engineering, for electronics and engineering, for organizational structure and opportunity, for parenting and family life, for the "schooling" process at all levels; and

    – avoid "front-and-center teaching and leading" as her primary modus operandi, thereby acknowledging in her teaching and leading approach that in high-performing classrooms the students' time-on-task (writing, computing, creating, discussing, planning) must outweigh the teacher's time-in-lecture (not to suggest that front-and-center teaching/leading should *necessarily* be reduced to a mere fraction of total in-class time, but that it should consistently total less than 50%).

These three examples are only that—examples. They illustrate some of the steps which teachers at various levels may consider taking in response to the 13 Teaching Characteristics shown and commented on in Chapter Two and the 22 second-tier Teaching Characteristics listed in Chapter Three.

Followship: Learned Optimism and True Grit

As noted in the previous chapter, a leadership position (such as that of a faculty member) does not automatically give one "followers"; it gives one "subordinates." Subordinates (i.e., students) become followers (i.e., learners) if superiors (i.e., faculty members) become leaders (i.e., teachers).

This chapter's title highlights leadership attitudes and behaviors that generate "followship" responses in students that tend to conform to a set of concepts originating in Dr. Martin Seligman's theories. These theories have also been used as a springboard to related research and formulations by many scholars and practitioners, notably Dr. Angela Duckworth. (Review Martin Seligman's seminal ideas in his classic work *Learned Optimism* and, even earlier, his *Psychopathology: Experimental Models*. Dr. Seligman is the author of the former; he edited and contributed to the latter. Angela Duckworth's innumerable published works include "Temperament in the Classroom," *Handbook of Temperament*, pp. 627–644.)

When applied to classrooms, Seligman's concepts imply that a teacher's response to a student moves that student toward "learned helplessness" or, alternatively, toward "learned optimism," depending on the response's characteristics and the tendencies of the student. When students see no connection between what they attempt and the apparent result, their mindset tends toward "learned helplessness." Conversely, when students see connections between what they attempt and the result, their mindset tends toward "learned optimism."

Learned helplessness is associated with lack of persistence and lack of determination (because there is no point in persisting when effort does not connect—in the student's mind—to outcomes). Learned optimism is associated with high levels of persistence and determination, and, thus, with resilience (because the student believes that continued effort eventually brings positive results).

Angela Duckworth's concept of "grit" layers itself nicely into the learned helplessness-learned optimism framework. She has found that grit ranks among the prime determinants of student success (ahead, in some contexts, even of intelligence). She defines grit as "sticking with things ... until you master them."

For the teacher, the key question about both learned optimism and grit is *Can these characteristics be taught and learned?* And the answer is *Yes, they can.* The trick is to provide students with such consistent and reliable reinforcement—positive or negative, as each instance merits, moment-to-moment—that they begin routinely to connect what they do with the (psychological) reward that their teacher(s) provides.

A number of the Teaching Characteristics cited in Chapters Two and Three have particular relevance. Several of them are repeated on the following pages.

Review each of these concepts, bearing in mind "learned optimism" and "gritty determination." Imagine how these teacher and leader behaviors might act on students, first to generate, and then draw out, the critical student characteristics of learned optimism (*the expectation that effort will reliably connect to result*) and grit (*the settled determination to stick with things until they are mastered*).

Teaching Characteristic Three: *I set clearly articulated standards for student academic performance.*

Comment: This is a statement not about your own scoring and grading system itself, but about your ability and willingness to illuminate the nature of your academic expectations, i.e., not about explaining that 90–93 = A- and 94–97 = A and 98–100 = A+, but delineating (in age-appropriate fashion, of course) the subject-specific levels of mastery that you expect from your students. An illustration of this might entail providing students with examples (in advance of an assignment) of submissions that you would grade as A, B, C, and so on, or involving your students in the development of the rubric.

Teaching Characteristic Ten: *I create predictable assessments (not to be confused with "simple" or "easy" assessments). My students can rely on the preparation that I offer them.*

Comment: This statement emphasizes the principle that assessments of any sort should reveal each student's grasp of facts, concepts, and their applications in problem-solving contexts, not their abilities either to guess what the teacher means, to deal with unexpected assessment formats, or to retrieve material that was not cited in assignments or in the review process. One of the surest ways to reduce levels of student performance, satisfaction, and enthusiasm is to assess students in ways that leave them consistently feeling "tricked." Students should feel, upon receiving their grade, that they had been told what format to expect, what material would be included, and the teacher's expectations (see Teaching Characteristic No. 3, "Comment"). While authentic assessments that require students to demonstrate learned skills in new contexts are excellent learning tools, students should know ahead of time that they will be asked to do this (if the context itself is not known). They should have had plenty of low-stakes practice applying skills to new contexts prior to the graded assessment.

Teaching Characteristic Eleven: *I provide fair, reliable, understandable grade and reward structures for my students. My students are led to understand why they receive the grades they receive—high or low—and thereby to see how improvement, if they will seek it, might be possible.*

Comment: While the words "fair," "reliable," and "understandable" connote this Teaching Characteristic's transparent relationship to "predictability," its relationship to "supportiveness" is even more critical. The simplest way to say this is that your feedback to your students on anything that is graded should leave them feeling *hopeful* that improvement might be possible. Your explicit comments—written or oral—on the steps needed to improve are considerably more important than the grade itself in this process. While the "improvement ball" always remains in your students' court, so to speak, the teacher's role must always include further instructions on the grip, the swing, the tactics, and the strategy. The least *and* the most academically successful students must feel an unquestioning confidence that you expect them to get better, from the first day of school to the last.

Among other first-tier (Chapter Two) characteristics, you may wish to review:

Teaching Characteristic One: *I find ways to make it obvious to all students that I wish them success every day, in and outside school.*

Teaching Characteristic Seven: *I demonstrate believably high levels of enthusiasm for teaching and learning and for the content of my studies.*

Among the second-tier (Chapter Three) characteristics, you may wish to review:

Teaching Characteristic Seventeen: *I am effective in establishing meaningful emotional and psychological engagement with all my students.*

Teaching Characteristic Twenty-One: *I am effective in providing private and public positive reinforcement for individual or group (student) successes.*

Now, having reviewed this smattering of the most pertinent Chapter Two and Chapter Three Teaching Characteristics, consider several classroom-specific examples as viewed through the student lens.

Suppose you are a ninth-grader, and suppose you submit an essay and form an expectation somehow that it is worth about a "B." It comes back a "C." The teacher's only written comments are (in your mind) vague and unhelpful (e.g., "Good effort, but slightly unfocused"). *You see no obvious connection between what you tried to do and the apparent result.* Learned helplessness has just been reinforced. Persistence (and thus performance, satisfaction, and enthusiasm) begins to diminish.

If you, the student, are "gritty" enough, you may have to endure many such unexplained disappointments before these characteristics—performance, satisfaction, and enthusiasm—begin to diminish. If you, the student, are not particularly "gritty," the onset of this decline may come fairly soon.

Note that it is *not* an issue of being given a grade that is lower than you hoped for, or expected, that has the debilitating influence on your future performance. Rather, it is *not having the teacher's rationale for the grade explained at all—or in a way that you can understand—that initiates the insidious decline.*

Now suppose you are a third-grader and that you decide to construct for your quarterly science project a diorama of the Colorado River's course, using a shoe box and clay. You bring it to school and your diorama takes its place among 20 other student projects. Your teacher gives blue ribbons to three of the projects. Yours is not one of them. Your science grade for the quarter is a "C." *You see no obvious connection between what you tried to do and the apparent result.*

Learned helplessness has just been reinforced. Persistence (and thus performance, satisfaction, and enthusiasm) begins to diminish.

Again, the issue is not the mediocre quality of your diorama. The issue is your teacher's having not taken the time to explain to you what exactly was good and not-so-good about your project. Words such as these can do wonders: "Next time, if you will try doing such-and-such, rather than such-and-such, I would expect your project to turn out quite nicely." (Please note the absence of any guarantee or promise of a better grade, but, rather, the simple commentary on the project's strengths and weaknesses, coupled with the forward view to something that might turn out better next time.)

Examples abound: You, as a student, come to class 10 minutes late and no negative reinforcement is forthcoming. You, as a student, do not prepare for your chemistry quiz, but your grade is as good as usual. You, as a student, *do* prepare with extraordinary care (by your own standards) for your math exam. But your grade, though improved in its raw score, is still the usual "C." Your classmates in general did better, too, and because the math teacher chose to "grade on the curve" (which is never recommended).

In each of these instances, you, the student, see no obvious connection between what you tried to do (or failed to do) and the apparent result. Learned helplessness has been reinforced. Persistence (and thus performance, satisfaction, and enthusiasm) begins to diminish.

You, the teacher, hold the key to reversing this deterioration. Note the expected deterioration is not just in student performance. It is, as well, in student satisfaction with, and enthusiasm for, the schooling experience. Note, too, that this has nothing to do with whether you, as a teacher, are viewed as "hard" or "easy."

So, to elicit consistently high-level performance (in the context, of course, of each student's native capacity) in your students, regardless of their age or grade level, concentrate on the thoroughgoing reinforcement that lets them know just where they are in your estimation, academically and behaviorally. Inspire them to work for high-level goals and simultaneously provide them with the positive and negative reinforcement necessary to help them get there. The teacher should provide clear, detailed feedback that invites action and revision on the part of the student.

The two caveats are (1) no "false positives"—no grade inflation solely "to make them feel good about themselves"—in your reinforcement, and (2) no instances of students being compared with each other (rather than with themselves over time).

Concerning the first caveat, this implies that students must *earn* their grades. Your challenge is to set up learning conditions so that they *can*, no matter how incrementally, experience some successes, whether large or small. But it is essential to not give false praise. Do not make the mistake of cheapening the value of your positive reinforcement.

The second caveat implies that students should be rewarded for their individual improvement (against your standards), rather than being rewarded only when performance surpasses that of their peers. This second caveat, as with nearly all recommendations that appear in this book, pertains specifically to classroom teaching and its ancillary activities of supervision in hallways, in lunchrooms, in after-school programs, and so on. This is not meant to discourage all competitive activities. Sports, music competition, science competition, competition for scholarships, and so on, can contribute usefully—*if coached, directed, and managed appropriately*—to the mission-related value of the overall schooling experience.

Anticipation and Renewal

What was your original impetus toward teaching as a possible career? What excited you about the prospect? What did you imagine in your mind's eye when you thought of yourself actually teaching? What really provided the motivation to prepare yourself, to seek a position, and to invest huge amounts of your effort and time—and money—into beginning this career?

Regardless of your current "stage" of career, what has become of those impetus generators? Are they still present, and in similar strength and proportion? Is your current reason-for-teaching compatible with the implications of the earlier chapters of this book? Will your current motivation be equal to the task of adopting these Teaching Characteristics and working toward excellence on each?

Depending on the stage of each teacher's career, certain faculty members may demonstrate the following qualities:

- preoccupation with family and leisure activities—certainly not a bad thing in itself—coupled with (however) a turning away from career interests, excitement, and motivation;

- marked reduction in earlier excitement about the intrinsic rewards found in teaching and guiding young people;

- loss of the *learned optimism* experienced regularly when faculty members were first mastering the teaching art, when they were more impressed by and excited about the connections they had begun to perceive between what they tried to do and the results of those efforts; and

- a perception of reduced career opportunity, a sense that fewer options await them on their career journeys.

If any of this describes you personally or if you observe this in others within the faculty on which you serve, then give considerable thought to the implications of the "ISM Faculty Experience Matrix," the diagram that appeared as Figure 3 in Chapter One. The likelihood is that without an ongoing faculty-endorsed culture of renewal, everyone—students, teachers, support staff, and administration—is simply "less" as a result: less high-performing, less satisfied, and less enthusiastic.

This is your career. You either move your career forward, or it tends toward stagnation. You move it forward by (a) maintaining high levels of *interest* in your fields of expertise—reading in professional journals, discussing concepts and techniques with peers, engaging in periodic formal study of various kinds—and (b) maintaining high levels of *involvement* in the lives of your students.

Set goals in both categories: your academic expertise *and* your involvement with students. You move toward the goals. As you move toward them, establish new ones. There is no limit to a teaching career's opportunities for learning. But more so than most careers, the career of the teacher is the prisoner of each individual teacher's own decisions about whether to let the career flourish or wither.

Renewal must become a fact of life in any organization for its individual and collective existence to become anything other than mundane. As a teacher, you will endeavor to make continuous learning a fact of life for your students.

What about for yourself? Consider some or all the ideas and suggestions that follow, and invent your own set. Some deal with the short term; others, with the long term of your entire career.

- Does setting "clearly articulated standards for student academic performance" or demonstrating "believably high levels of enthusiasm ... for the content of my studies" (see Teaching Characteristics No. 3 and 7 in Chapter Two) seem too much of a stretch at this stage of your career? What would happen if you arranged to observe (more than once) a colleague—on your faculty or on some other faculty—whose reputation for inspiring students in these ways is substantial?

- Is staying on the "cutting edge" too much trouble (see Teaching Characteristics No. 14, 15, 16, 27, and 28 in Chapter Three)? What would happen if you and several colleagues formed a "Mathematics Breakfast Club" or an "After-hours (Children's) Literature Study" or an every-faculty-meeting "Reading Theory Colloquium"?

- Do increased levels of outside-of-class involvement with students (see Teaching Characteristics No. 18 and 19 in Chapter Three) strike you as a burden? What would happen if you initiated something on your own terms? For example, rather than volunteering to coordinate the next field trip—something requiring months of planning—suppose you offered to conduct periodic after-school or evening sessions on something in which you have both interest and informal expertise, say, Meteorology or Nutrition or Behavioral Health? Bear in mind that "involvement" is the operative word. Making an occasional *presentation* probably would not fit. Scraping together half-dozen inexpensive telescopes periodically and chatting with students and parents about planets and stars and galaxies certainly would.

- Consider crafting at least the outline of a career-long professional development plan. The plan should include formal study in your field(s) at least every 36–48 months. This can be for graduate credit or not for graduate credit, but it should, above all, be *interesting, meaningful, and exciting to you*. Otherwise, do not bother. "Credit" and "meaning" are not necessarily related to each other.

- Your professional growth plan should thoroughly and thoughtfully dovetail with the plans of at least one of your colleagues on the faculty. By coordinating these plans yourselves, you multiply your efforts. You learn from one another.

- Your professional growth plan should connect you with your original impetus for entering the teaching field. Often that original impetus was laced with idealism. *Recapture that in some "more mature" version*. Your plan will display more realism and pragmatism than any plan you could have written earlier, no matter where you are now in your career development, but it should not ignore that seminal idealism which led you initially to the classroom.

- Your professional growth plan should include self-rewards. The further you develop in your profession, the less likely you are (in many schools) to receive positive reinforcement from your administration, no matter how excellent its members may be. Your competence becomes "assumed." So, rather than developing *learned helplessness* because you see no connection between your efforts and your administrators' acknowledgment of those efforts, build *self-reinforcement* into your *self-renewal* plan. Make sure you and your peers, for example, regularly reinforce one another (but, as with the students, only when reinforcement is actually *earned*). Make sure your plan is written, so that you can monitor your progress in a formal way. Share what you learn through a workshop or course with your colleagues and request of your administrators that this be the expectation for all teachers.

The goal is to see the connections between your efforts and their outcomes. Learned optimism implies writing a professional development plan, following that plan, and rewarding yourself systematically as you reach its various targets. Your results are the same as the results for your students when you lead them to experience learned optimism: *persistence, performance, satisfaction, and enthusiasm*.

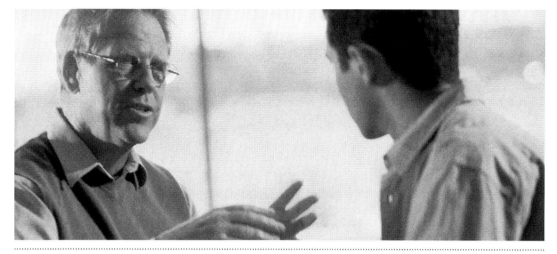

Parenting—Home and School

The best teachers have always parented. Regardless of their students' ages, they have parented. Regardless of their students' socioeconomic backgrounds, they have parented. Regardless of the subject matter, they have parented.

That is, the best teachers have *engaged* their students in life-shaping ways and at life-changing levels. By example and by persuasion—overt or subtle—they have stamped their students with an unmistakable imprint: personal responsibility, maturity, integrity, and loyalty.

This engaged-teacher role has been critical for countless students. Many students come from families with dual-working parents or single-parent families. In those and other families, the ubiquitous televisions, computers, and handheld electronic devices are all busily "teaching" their own values, nonvalues, and antivalues. This often leaves teachers as collectively the best-positioned individuals in society to deliver those four classic parental values: personal responsibility, maturity, integrity, and loyalty. The state of the family now implies that teachers, as a body of professionals, must consider classroom parenting a basic, indispensable component of their calling.

The concepts of "learned helplessness" and "learned optimism"—as crucial factors in a given student's persistence, performance, satisfaction, and enthusiasm levels—have been described at length throughout this workbook. Now consider those concepts in the context of the relationship between home and school.

If the at-home parents (as distinct from the teachers-as-parents) define "success" for their children only as perfection or as being "first," their reinforcement program will not match yours (provided you are using the Teaching Characteristics recommended in Chapters Two and Three). You will be reinforcing incremental improvements demonstrated by the student, regardless of the student's distance from perfection or from "first place." In a student facing this contradiction, learned helplessness at home will compete with the learned optimism you are developing at school. The net impact on a given student's persistence, performance, satisfaction, and enthusiasm is not predictable.

Similarly, if the at-home parents (as distinct from the teachers-as-parents) are totally nonreinforcing, perhaps because they are more interested in being "friends" with their children than in guiding them, the two reinforcement programs again will not match. For a given student facing this inconsistency, the net impact on that student's persistence, performance, satisfaction, and enthusiasm is not predictable, any more than in the first instance.

What does this imply? Simply that if you and your colleagues implement the Teaching Characteristics advocated in this workbook at a level approaching true excellence, so learned optimism is rampant at your school, you *still* may lose some of your students to the counterbalancing forces of their at-home parents.

Angela Duckworth's concept of "gritty persistence" in your students exists, of course, as the other wild card which you can only influence, rather than control. No matter what you and your colleagues do, persistence, performance, satisfaction, and enthusiasm may still deteriorate in some of your students.

In lower-school, self-contained classrooms in which you are the teacher with whom your students spend most of every day, a Parent Education Plan (PEP)—whether devised by you alone for your students' parents or devised by your faculty-administration as a schoolwide effort—is potentially significant. A PEP that communicates to parents in lay terms what you hope to accomplish may help your students encounter mutually reinforcing strategies at home and at school.

Consider, for example, the implications within a PEP of Teaching Characteristics such as No. 4 ("I set reasonable, defensible standards for student behavior") or No. 12 ("I enforce our rules justly, fairly, and consistently") or No. 13 ("I am able to present myself each day in ways that will be seen by my students as consistent and reliable, i.e., unaffected by outside-of-school problems") or No. 24 ("I am effective in establishing proactive communication with, and service to, each student's parents"). Imagine a PEP that explicates and illustrates for your lower-school parents the meaning of such characteristics. Parents who choose private schools for their children are usually (not always, of course) willing learners. Educate them. Give them the chance to reinforce their children at home with approaches similar to those you employ at school.

For middle- and upper-school students whose daily contact with you may be less than one hour (because of your departmentalized schedule), the importance of a faculty-wide approach becomes especially critical. A student who, for example, encounters but one teacher per day who uses the 13 Teaching Characteristics spelled out in Chapter Two of this workbook, and who then faces five who do not (and, as well, a set of at-home parents who also do not) would need to have a stunning measure of Duckworth's "gritty" determination to maintain consistent performance, strong levels of satisfaction, and genuine enthusiasm, no matter what you—acting alone—can do.

But if a given student, hour-after-hour, day-after-day, and year-after-year, encounters a unified faculty culture that reinforces in her or him developing learning habits and behavioral responses consistent with this workbook's Teaching Characteristics, the chances of counterbalancing nonsupportive at-home parenting may change from marginal to good. And if, through an appropriate schoolwide PEP, parental support is enlisted for the entire endeavor, the percentage of learned-helpless students in your school can be expected to be small indeed.

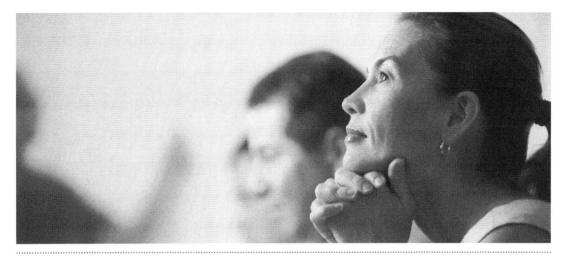

Revisiting Your Academic Roots

Think back.

Try to remember your first true experience of *intellectual* excitement.

Was it rooted in dinosaurs in 4th grade? Geography in the 8th? Biology in the 9th? Geometry in the 10th? Literature in the 12th?

Or are you unwilling to call any of those excitements "intellectual"? Do you have to move mentally to your college years to find your first intellectual excitement?

And where did you find that? In physics? In calculus? In philosophy? In French literature?

Or was it in theology, chemistry, or world history?

Or, if you studied pedagogy, did that first intellectual excitement occur when you examined developmental reading theory for the first time, and began to draw for yourself a portrait of how a child's mind first grapples with written symbols?

Wherever that experience was and however young or old you were, recall the characteristics of the event or events. What—exactly—intrigued you? How were the ideas delivered to your mind? What seeds were planted inside you then?

If the experience developed in a classroom, what made you actually look forward to the next meeting of the class? What made you reflect on the class after it ended and you no longer "had" to think about it?

Pause now for just a moment, if you will. Look away from the page and remember that early eagerness to know more. Picture the people immersed with you in that endeavor: the teacher or professor, your classmates, perhaps your parents. Remember how you imagined yourself going forward with your life from that point, with your perspectives altered and your mind opened by new patterns and new paradigms.

Now think back again, but not as far (presumably) into the past.

Try to remember your LAST encounter with intellectual excitement.

Not the last time you *provided* intellectual excitement for your students (important though that certainly is), but the last time you yourself *experienced* the kind of intellectual excitement you recalled just 30 seconds ago.

If you are in the same situation as that in which many teachers find themselves, your most recent experience of true intellectual excitement is not particularly recent. It is a more distant memory.

Think about that paradox. To teach well by the principles developed in ISM's studies and presented in this workbook, inspiring your students is a fundamental component in developing persistence, strong performance, high levels of satisfaction, and sustained enthusiasm in those students. In turn, renewing your "professional self" is a fundamental component in maintaining persistence, strong performance, high levels of satisfaction, and sustained enthusiasm in *yourself*.

Recall the following items from Chapters Two and Three of this workbook:

Teaching Characteristic Seven: *I demonstrate believably high levels of enthusiasm for teaching/learning and for the content of my studies.*

Teaching Characteristic Fourteen: *I pursue career-long professional development as a foremost priority.*

Teaching Characteristic Fifteen: *I am current and knowledgeable about pedagogical science and my content area.*

Teaching Characteristic Sixteen: *I have mastered at least one pedagogical approach that is supported by reliable, contemporary research outcomes.*

Teaching Characteristic Twenty-Seven: *I am effective in communicating in-class experimentation-and-testing outcomes and findings to colleagues, within and beyond the school.*

Teaching Characteristic Twenty-Eight: *I participate regularly in outside-the-school academic organizations whose work is supportive of, and pertinent to, my field(s).*

Consider all six Teaching Characteristics. Think about the implied relationships among them. They bespeak enthusiasm for:

- teaching and learning;
- the content of your material;
- teaching development as a priority;
- current methodology and theory;
- research-supported teaching methods;

- in-your-own-classroom experimentation;
- "cross-pollination" with colleagues within and beyond your school; and
- participation in relevant-to-you academic organizations and associations.

We know the adage, "a rising tide lifts all boats." Certainly, you can "renew your professional self" as a solo activity, simply as a step in reinforcing in yourself the high levels of performance, satisfaction, and enthusiasm that we know to be associated with the strongest student and faculty cultures. But we also know that linking yourself to a colleague, or to several colleagues, or to your academic department, or to your lower-, middle-, and upper-school division teachers, or to your whole-school faculty, or to academic organizations beyond your school—any or all of these steps—is likely to make your long-term self-renewal more certain and more gratifying.

This is why each of the self-rating scales in Chapters Two and Three took you beyond rating your current level to that of your three-year goal as well as to that of your faculty colleagues (in your own estimation). Working alone or with colleagues, set out to recapture something of the seminal enthusiasm that led you to this profession.

There is a sense in which this should become part of the "due diligence" of the vocation itself. It is simply not enough to coast forward in this career, having mastered the rudiments of teaching and having reached a level of intellectual and pedagogical competence.

Your students—and you—deserve much, much more.

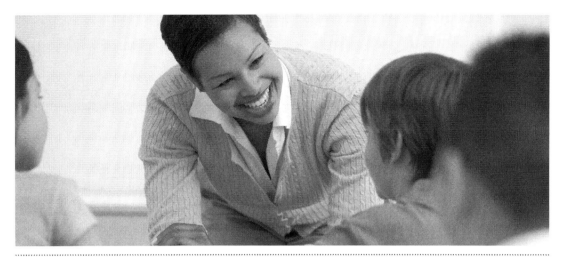

Community: Assessments

Your adherence, or not, to the teaching approaches necessary to create and sustain a "predictable and supportive" environment often reveals itself clearly in your approach to assessment creation, assessment giving, and scoring and grading. Three of the Teaching Characteristics shown in Chapter Two are especially pertinent here. Because each of these characteristics is easily misunderstood or misinterpreted, the "Comment" for each is included.

Teaching Characteristic Three: *I set clearly articulated standards for student academic performance.*

Comment: This is a statement *not* about your own scoring and grading system itself. It is about your ability and willingness to illuminate the nature of your academic expectations, i.e., *not* about explaining that 90–93 = A- and 94–97 = A and 98–100 = A+, but delineating (in age-appropriate fashion, of course) the subject-specific levels of mastery that you expect from your students. An illustration of this might entail providing students with examples (before an assignment) of submissions that you would grade as A, B, C, and so on, or involving your students in the development of the rubric.

Teaching Characteristic Ten: *I create predictable* **assessments** *(not to be confused either with "simple" or "easy"* **assessments***). My students can rely on the preparation that I offer them.*

Comment: This statement emphasizes the principle that tests of any sort should reveal each student's grasp of facts, concepts, and their applications in problem-solving contexts. It is *not* about their abilities either to guess what the teacher means, to deal with unexpected testing formats, or to retrieve material that was not cited in assignments or in the test-review process.

One of the surest ways to reduce levels of student performance, satisfaction, and enthusiasm is to test students in ways that leave them consistently feeling "tricked." Students shouldfeel, upon receiving their grades, that they had been told what testing format to expect, what material would be included, and the teacher's expectations (see Teaching Characteristic No. 3, "Comment"). While authentic assessments that require students to demonstrate learned skills in new contexts are excellent learning tools, students should know ahead of time that they will be asked to do this (if the context itself is not known). They should have had plenty of low-stakes practice applying skills to new contexts prior to the graded assessment.

Teaching Characteristic Eleven: *I provide fair, reliable, understandable grade and reward structures for my students. My students are led to understand why they receive the grades they receive—high or low—and thereby to see how improvement, if they will seek it, might be possible.*

Comment: While the words "fair," "reliable," and "understandable" connote this Teaching Characteristic's transparent relationship to "predictability," its relationship to "supportiveness" is even more critical. The simplest way to say this is that your feedback to your students on anything that is graded should leave them feeling *hopeful* that improvement might be possible. Your explicit comments—written or oral—on the steps needed to improve are considerably more important than the grade itself in this process. While the "improvement ball" always remains in your students' court, so to speak, the teacher's role must always include further instructions on the grip, the swing, the tactics, and the strategy. The least *and* the most academically successful of your students must feel an unquestioning confidence that you expect them to get better, from the first day of school to the last.

Assessment and grading, on the one hand, and teaching and learning, on the other, sometimes dovetail so thoroughly that it is hard to envision where one ends and the other begins. Examples come readily to mind.

Picture a skillfully taught third-year foreign language class. In such a setting, assessment and teaching often become indistinguishable as the teacher assists, cajoles, prods, hints, and shares in the daily translation process, all the while making judgments about both the students' progress toward excellence and about the quality and effectiveness of his or her own instructional approach.

Now imagine a third-grade reading session conducted by a skilled veteran. Once more, assessment and teaching become indistinguishable from each other, as the teacher simultaneously assists the students, makes judgments about the students, and makes judgments about the effectiveness of his or her own instructional process.

These have in common simultaneous *helping and assessing activities* by a skilled teacher.

It is this continual process of providing positive and negative reinforcement, day after day, hour after hour, minute after minute, which establishes clear connections in students' minds between what they do and the results of what they do. As emphasized earlier in this workbook, it is this clarity of cause-and-effect connection in students' minds that is associated with the persistence, performance, satisfaction, and enthusiasm that most teachers hope to develop—and to develop *deliberately*—in their students.

At least as important, though, this continual attention to the blending of teaching and assessing provides *the teacher* with evidence of cause-effect connection, which is just as critical to her or him as to the students. Where this connection is reinforced daily, the teacher, too, is more likely to maintain high levels of *instructional* persistence, performance, and personal and professional satisfaction and enthusiasm.

In environments wherein learned optimism is generated consistently by the faculty and in which, consequently, the sense of community is strong, even the most unsuccessful students tend to declare confidently that teachers makes clear to them what they should do to move toward mastery. They also declare themselves secure in their certainty that their teachers are on their side, and declare that, once they decide to "get in gear," everything will be fine. (They may, at the same time, acknowledge the possibility that they will never choose to "get in gear.")

Conversely, in environments in which learned helplessness is generated consistently by the faculty and in which, consequently, the sense of community is weak, the most successful of students will assert that they succeed *despite* the faculty—in Angela Duckworth's terms, they succeed only as a result of their "gritty determination." They are also certain beyond question that their success or failure is of interest to their teachers *only* in the sense that, when they graduate and move to the next level of schooling, their teachers will take interest and pride in their acceptance into a strong institution.

This latter situation is not necessarily a terrible state of affairs. But it is nonetheless regrettable. It is regrettable in that both teachers and students will have performed at levels well below their individual capacities, will have experienced satisfaction levels well below those they might have known, and will have felt far less enthusiasm for their school experience than that which was within their collective reach.

Community: Responsibility

ISM's studies over a period of two decades and ISM's experience in schools over a period of four decades have pointed to a set of relationships between teachers and students—students of any age—that are psychologically and emotionally healthy. In schools in which student performance, satisfaction, and enthusiasm are strong, teachers have tended to have high academic expectations of their students, yes. But they have also tended to display conspicuously high levels of supportiveness for their students' efforts.

Hand-in-hand with that teacher supportiveness go an excitement about, a commitment to, and an immersion in, students' academic and cocurricular progress that appear to relegate "control"—for its own sake—to the back row. These teachers, paradoxically enough, are just too busy with their basic professional reasons-for-being to invest huge amounts of time and energy in behavioral minutiae.

They are so prepared, so organized, so focused, so excited about what they are teaching—and so committed to getting their students "on task" while in class—they just cannot take the view that every behavioral irregularity must be confronted and beaten down. They can, in short, be "taken advantage of" in small ways without feeling a great deal of concern about that fact.

There tends to be a grudging good-naturedness about these teachers' expectations of their students' behaviors. There tends to be a willingness to say, at least implicitly, "If you work as hard as I expect, I will give you a *little* leeway behaviorally, especially in your interactions with your peers."

This should not be taken as an indication that a *laissez-faire* approach to classroom behavior control is being recommended. The emphasis here is, rather, on the rationality and defensibleness of your behavioral expectations, and the good-naturedness with which you apply those expectations.

Recall the language of Teaching Characteristic Four in Chapter Two of this workbook. And note especially the "Comment" paragraph.

Teaching Characteristic Four: *I set reasonable, defensible standards for student behavior.*

Comment: This is a statement *not* about schoolwide rules and regulations, but about the behavioral expectations you develop with and for students in your own classroom. The statement implies that your behavioral expectations should be spelled out—possibly in writing and posted in your classroom—and, beyond that, worded in ways that are intelligible to your students. (It is worth remembering that "bad laws make hard cases." Your standards for student behavior in your classroom should relate to the school mission and should be viewed by students as *reasonable* applications of that mission.) As a community-building opportunity at the beginning of the year, consider involving your students in the development of classroom rules, etiquette, and expectations.

Picture a middle-school hallway between classes. Controlled chaos reigns. Teachers who will demand courteously, two minutes from now, that their students sit down promptly and immediately prepare their desks for *work,* now comfortably watch students being kid-like, intervening only when safety or decibel issues require.

This benign tolerance for hallway goofiness changes into a focused expectation—convertible in a heartbeat to a courteous demand, if necessary—that every student's attention is snapped onto the teacher for start-of-academic business. This takes sustained, daily practice on the part of both teachers and students, as does everything that you wish to become habitual in yourself and your students.

The alternatives to "context-determined behavioral expectations" do not work. If the hallway looseness continues into the classroom's academic environment, performance suffers. If lock-step behavior is required in the middle-school hallway, a sense of oppression will prevail. The results of *either* of these are predictable: a weak sense of community, little success in teaching the meaning of responsibility and adult-like behavior, and plenty of student-teacher tension.

Student performance—for any age or grade level—flourishes when students are treated by their teachers in ways that:

(a) enhance their self-perceived worth;

(b) demonstrate their teachers' high expectations (including expectations for an age-appropriate version of "adult-like behavior"); and

(c) communicate the idea that their teachers are "on their side" and "desire their success" (and yet demand focused commitment to the academic task at hand).

Review and Conclusion

Chapter Two—before its display of the 13 top-tier Teaching Characteristics—noted the following. Take a moment to review, keeping in mind that there is no single "correct" way to use the material in this workbook. Here are a few of your choices.

- Work through the material as an individual, using the workbook-like pages to score yourself, to reach decisions about changes in your own approach that you might wish to attempt, and to set professional development goals for yourself.

- Do the same in cooperation with one or more of your peers, meeting periodically to discuss these ideas, to initiate individual or small-group (pedagogical) trials—a form of "action research"—and to compare notes week-by-week and month-by-month.

- Involve your administrator(s) to:

    (a) perform a whole-faculty self-scoring on the ISM Faculty Experience Survey and Scoring Chart (Appendix A);

    (b) discuss the outcomes vis-à-vis the ISM Faculty Experience Matrix (shown previously in Chapter One);

    (c) administer the Student Experience Profile (Appendix B);

    (d) administer the Faculty Culture Profile (Appendix C); and

    (e) in other creative ways, integrate your own work in this book with the in-parallel work of your colleagues, with the long-term goal of establishing and maintaining your faculty culture's position in the upper-right quadrant of the ISM Faculty Experience Matrix.

You are now in better position to understand those three bullet points—and their implications—than when you first read them in Chapter Two. And so you have a sense of how quickly you can multiply the whole-school effects of implementation of these teaching characteristics when that implementation rises above the single-teacher level to the faculty peer-group level (e.g., grade level, department level) to the divisional level to the whole-faculty level. And it is at these latter levels—the divisional level and the whole-faculty level—that it becomes meaningful to speak of *the faculty culture*. At those levels, your school's students, and you, begin to experience those qualities listed in the optimal quadrant of the ISM Faculty Experience Matrix.

And there, operating within a fully "predictable and supportive" environment, your school's students—all of them—will be afforded the finest possible conditions under which to maximize their performance, satisfaction, and enthusiasm, one student at a time. And the same will be true of their teachers.

ISM Faculty Experience Survey and Scoring Instructions

The questions in this faculty culture survey are based on ISM's findings in the Student Experience Study (SES), which indicated primary predictors of student performance, satisfaction, and enthusiasm. As opposed to a faculty satisfaction survey, ISM's focus in this survey is on the overall climate or culture of the school—as opposed to a focus on the individual.

Each question begins with the phrase, **"I and my colleagues ..."** Though you cannot speak with complete accuracy for your colleagues, what interests us for the purpose of this survey is your perspective on the issues and *your impressions* of your colleagues' perspectives on the issues.

ISM Faculty Experience Survey

Circle only one number for each item. Consider in your responses only the three most recent months unless otherwise instructed.

1. I and my colleagues understand exactly how we are evaluated.

1	2	3	4	5	6	7	8	9
(Not true at all)								*(Exactly True)*

2. I and my colleagues view our evaluation procedures as consistent (i.e., predictable).

1	2	3	4	5	6	7	8	9
(Not true at all)								*(Exactly True)*

3. I and my colleagues view our evaluation procedures as constructive (i.e., helpful).

1	2	3	4	5	6	7	8	9
(Not true at all)								*(Exactly True)*

4. I and my colleagues view our faculty culture as appropriately supportive (as evidenced by collegial interaction).

1	2	3	4	5	6	7	8	9
(Not true at all)								*(Exactly True)*

5. I and my colleagues view our school's administrative culture (i.e., the collective attitude of all our administrative staff members, including those in the Business Office, Development Office, Admission Office, and so on) as appropriately supportive of the faculty, i.e., wishing our success and striving to support us in our efforts.

| 1 | 2 | 3 | 4 | 5 | 6 | 7 | 8 | 9 |

(Not true at all)   *(Exactly True)*

6. I and my colleagues find that the administrator(s) who supervises and evaluates us is highly supportive of us, i.e., hopes for our success and is focused on our growth and renewal as professionals.

| 1 | 2 | 3 | 4 | 5 | 6 | 7 | 8 | 9 |

(Not true at all)   *(Exactly True)*

7. I and my colleagues agree that the administrator(s) who supervises and evaluates us provides us with accurate reinforcement regarding our performance as faculty members.

| 1 | 2 | 3 | 4 | 5 | 6 | 7 | 8 | 9 |

(Not true at all)   *(Exactly True)*

8. I and my colleagues agree that the administrator(s) who supervises and evaluates us demonstrates consistent responses on a daily basis. We find that we know what to expect from her/him in all situations.

| 1 | 2 | 3 | 4 | 5 | 6 | 7 | 8 | 9 |

(Not true at all)   *(Exactly True)*

9. I and my colleagues agree that the administrator(s) who supervises us and evaluates us provides clarity of expectations.

| 1 | 2 | 3 | 4 | 5 | 6 | 7 | 8 | 9 |

(Not true at all)   *(Exactly True)*

10. I and my colleagues agree that the administrator(s) who supervises us and evaluates us is eager to assist us in meeting those expectations.

| 1 | 2 | 3 | 4 | 5 | 6 | 7 | 8 | 9 |

(Not true at all)   *(Exactly True)*

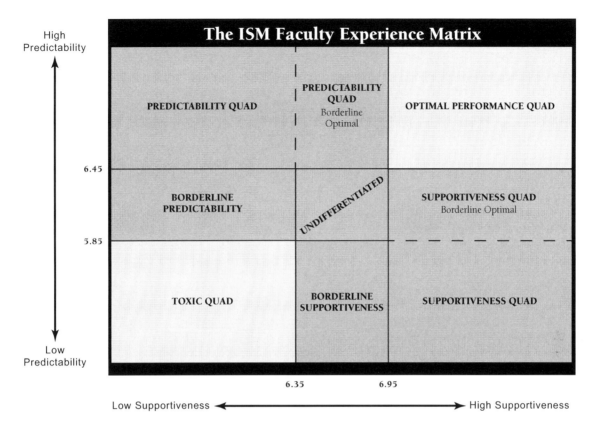

Scoring Instructions

A. Determine your faculty's (or your faculty unit's) mean score for each of the 10 items.

B. Average the mean scores for items 3, 4, 5, 6, and 10.

C. Go to the ISM Faculty Experience Matrix Scoring Chart (above), and on the horizontal "supportiveness" axis, circle the nearest whole number to reflect your average or mean.

D. Average the mean scores for items 1, 2, 7, 8, and 9.

E. Go to the ISM Faculty Experience Matrix Scoring Chart, and on the vertical "predictability" axis, circle the nearest whole number to reflect your average/mean.

F. At the intersection of the vertical and horizontal axis scores, place a star to indicate your faculty's self-placement on the ISM Faculty Experience Matrix. Then make reference to the ISM Faculty Experience Matrix itself (see Chapter One), where you will find lists of the general characteristics to be expected in each of the quadrants.

Note: After collecting data from three years of administering this survey, our research department established norms based on the responses of thousands of teachers. When placing your results on the matrix, note that predictability scores above 6.45 and below 5.85, and supportiveness scores above 6.95 or below 6.35, determine whether your score falls in the optimal or toxic end of those factors, respectively.

Comment: Although the quadrant-placement concept is derived from decades of ISM research into faculty and student cultures, the quadrant-placement scoring system itself is not a research outcome. Use your quadrant-placement outcomes to extend the faculty-culture conversation with your teachers. Emphasize the statistical relationship between faculty culture characteristics and student culture characteristics and, thus, with student performance, satisfaction, and enthusiasm.

ISM Student Experience Profile

Your school's results from the ISM Student Experience Profile should, ISM suggests, serve as one basis for ongoing professional-development-focused conversations with individual teachers and, as well, with whole-faculty groups and subgroups. (Note: this instrument was developed within grade 5–12 contexts, and is designed for use by students in those grade levels, inclusive.)

Circle only one number for each item. Consider only the most recent grading period in your responses.

1. I have very much looked forward to coming to school every day of this grading period.

| 1 | 2 | 3 | 4 | 5 | 6 | 7 | 8 | 9 |

Not true of me at all)   Exactly true of me

2. I have not seen or heard of unkind behavior—of anybody being "picked on" in any way at all— anywhere in our school during this grading period.

| 1 | 2 | 3 | 4 | 5 | 6 | 7 | 8 | 9 |

Absolutely no unkind behavior   Unkind behavior every day

3. I find that I am proud of my school and proud to be part of such a school.

| 1 | 2 | 3 | 4 | 5 | 6 | 7 | 8 | 9 |

Not true of me at all   Exactly true of me

*4. It has been obvious to me that my teachers **really** want me to do well—in school and out of school.*

| 1 | 2 | 3 | 4 | 5 | 6 | 7 | 8 | 9 |

Not accurate at all   Fully accurate

5. My teachers have worked every day at helping me become a better, more ethical person, regardless of the subject they are teaching (math, science, English, history, etc.).

1	2	3	4	5	6	7	8	9

Not accurate at all   Fully accurate

6. I have been very excited about what I've been studying this grading period (the course material itself, not the teaching of the material).

1	2	3	4	5	6	7	8	9

No, zero excitement   Yes, tremendous excitement

7. I'm so satisfied with my school, I'd certainly want to come here if my family and I could choose again.

1	2	3	4	5	6	7	8	9

No, absolutely not   Yes, certainly

8. Our assessments (tests, quizzes, etc.) this grading period have included exactly what my teachers said they would include.

1	2	3	4	5	6	7	8	9

No, our teachers always tried to trick us   Yes, our assessments covered exactly what we were told to study

9. All the grades I received during this grading period—tests, quizzes, papers, etc.—were exactly the grades I think I actually earned—no higher or lower.

1	2	3	4	5	6	7	8	9

Never the correct grade   Always the correct grade

10. I have been completely satisfied with our rules.

1	2	3	4	5	6	7	8	9

Terrible, senseless rules   Perfectly appropriate rules

11. *Our teachers have enforced our rules (including the dress code) justly, fairly, and consistently.*

| 1 | 2 | 3 | 4 | 5 | 6 | 7 | 8 | 9 |

Unfair or no enforcement   *Fair, just enforcement*

12. *I have known exactly what to expect from my teachers every day. I have known just how they will react to anything we say or do.*

| 1 | 2 | 3 | 4 | 5 | 6 | 7 | 8 | 9 |

Teachers moody and unpredictable   *Teachers perfectly consistent every day*

To score the Student Experience Profile so as to make outcomes comparable to this study's outcomes, break each student's scores into the three scales: Predictability and Support scale: items 2, 4, 5, 8, 9, 11, 12 (item 2 reverse scored); Satisfaction scale: items 1, 7, 10; Enthusiasm scale: items 1, 3, 6. (Item 1 is double-scored.) Thus, for a given student, the P/S scale's maximum score is 63 (9 x 7 items); the Satisfaction and Enthusiasm scales' maximum scores are 27 each (9 x 3 items).

ISM Faculty Culture Profile

This faculty culture instrument links strongly to the ISM findings in the Student Experience Study regarding student performance, student satisfaction, and student enthusiasm. Your own school's outcomes from the two instruments may profitably be considered companion pieces in your ongoing efforts to monitor the extent to which "predictability and support" conditions are present, and how strongly so, within your teaching and learning environment. (ISM recommends that the Faculty Culture Profile be given in fall, winter, and spring, with an Evaluation Design Team of exemplary teachers administering the instrument and assisting faculty leaders and administrators in the interpretation of the outcomes, item-by-item.)

Part A: Faculty culture items related to the Student Experience Profile

Circle only one number for each item.

Consider only the most recent grading period in your responses unless otherwise directed.

1. *I and my colleagues find ways to make it obvious to all students that we wish them success every day, in and outside of school.*

1	2	3	4	5	6	7	8	9

Not true of us at all   *Exactly true of us*

2. *I and my colleagues find ways to make it obvious to all students that we want them to become better, more ethical people (in ways consistent with our school's stated purposes and projected outcomes for our graduates).*

1	2	3	4	5	6	7	8	9

Not true of us at all   *Exactly true of us*

3. *I and my colleagues set clearly articulated standards for student academic performance.*

1	2	3	4	5	6	7	8	9

Not true of us at all   *Exactly true of us*

4. I and my colleagues set reasonable, defensible standards for student behavior.

| 1 | 2 | 3 | 4 | 5 | 6 | 7 | 8 | 9 |

Not true of us at all   Exactly true of us

---

5. I and my colleagues are continually alert to displays of unkindness between and among our students.

| 1 | 2 | 3 | 4 | 5 | 6 | 7 | 8 | 9 |

Not true of us at all   Exactly true of us

---

6. In confrontations with students, I and my colleagues conduct ourselves in ways that leave students' dignity intact regardless of the nature of the issue or infraction.

1   2   3   4   5   6   7   8   9

Not true of us at all   Exactly true of us

---

7. I and my colleagues individually and collectively demonstrate believably high levels of enthusiasm for teaching and learning and for the content of our studies.

| 1 | 2 | 3 | 4 | 5 | 6 | 7 | 8 | 9 |

Not true of us at all   Exactly true of us

---

8. I and my colleagues demonstrate through words and actions a genuine, believable commitment to the school, its purposes, its leadership, and each other.

| 1 | 2 | 3 | 4 | 5 | 6 | 7 | 8 | 9 |

Not true of us at all   Exactly true of us

9. I and my colleagues are glad to arrive at school and to see our students each day.

| 1 | 2 | 3 | 4 | 5 | 6 | 7 | 8 | 9 |

Not true of us at all   *Exactly true of us*

10. I and my colleagues create predictable assessments (not to be confused either with "simple" or with "easy" assessments). Our students can rely on the preparation we offer them.

| 1 | 2 | 3 | 4 | 5 | 6 | 7 | 8 | 9 |

Not true of us at all   *Exactly true of us*

11. I and my colleagues provide fair, reliable, understandable grade and reward structures for our students. Our students are led to understand why they receive the grades they receive—high or low—and thereby to see how improvement, if they will seek it, might be possible.

| 1 | 2 | 3 | 4 | 5 | 6 | 7 | 8 | 9 |

Not true of us at all   *Exactly true of us*

12. I and my colleagues enforce our rules justly, fairly, and consistently.

| 1 | 2 | 3 | 4 | 5 | 6 | 7 | 8 | 9 |

Not true of us at all   *Exactly true of us*

13. I and my colleagues are able to present ourselves each day in ways that will be seen by our students as consistent and reliable (i.e., unaffected by outside-of-school problems).

| 1 | 2 | 3 | 4 | 5 | 6 | 7 | 8 | 9 |

Not true of us at all   *Exactly true of us*

Part B: Selected faculty culture items related to the original ISM study of students and teachers

14. I and my colleagues individually and collectively pursue career-long professional development as a foremost priority.

1	2	3	4	5	6	7	8	9

Not true of us at all   Exactly true of us

15. I and my colleagues have mastered at least one pedagogical approach—not necessarily the same one for all of us—that is supported by reliable, contemporary research outcomes.

1	2	3	4	5	6	7	8	9

Not true of us at all   Exactly true of us

16. When I and my colleagues are in casual conversations with each other, those conversations tend to be constructive, upbeat, and professional.

1	2	3	4	5	6	7	8	9

Not true of us at all   Exactly true of us

17. I and my colleagues have great respect for our division and school administrators.

1	2	3	4	5	6	7	8	9

Not true of us at all   Exactly true of us

18. I and my colleagues find that our division and school administrators are highly supportive of our division's and school's faculty.

1	2	3	4	5	6	7	8	9

Not true of us at all   Exactly true of us

19. *I and my colleagues find that our division and school administrators are highly supportive of our division's and school's students.*

1	2	3	4	5	6	7	8	9

Not true of us at all   *Exactly true of us*

20. *I and my colleagues find that our division and school administrators are highly supportive of our division's and school's parents.*

1	2	3	4	5	6	7	8	9

Not true of us at all   *Exactly true of us*

Scores of 7, 8, and 9 are considered at the "good end" of the scale. You should be looking to attain a goal of 75% of scores of 7, 8, and 9 on each statement. Regardless of the outcomes, discuss those statements with lower scores with your colleagues and administrators to identify causes and solutions.

Made in the USA
Columbia, SC
12 May 2020